WORKBOOK

ICON

International Communication
Through English

Donald Freeman

Kathleen Graves

Linda Lee

 McGraw-Hill

P9-DXH-383

ICON International Communication through English, 1st Edition

Published by McGraw-Hill ESL/ELT, a business unit of The McGraw-Hill Companies, Inc. 1221 Avenue of the Americas, New York, NY 10020. Copyright © 2005 by The McGraw-Hill Companies, Inc. All rights reserved. No part of this publication may be reproduced or distributed in any form or by any means, or stored in a database or retrieval system, without the prior written consent of The McGraw-Hill Companies, Inc., including, but not limited to, in any network or other electronic storage or transmission, or broadcast for distance learning.

ISBN: 0-07-255040-6
  2 3 4 5 6 7 8 9 10 VL 09 08 07 06 05

ISE ISBN: 0-07-111725-3
1 2 3 4 5 6 7 8 9 10 VL 09 08 07 06 05 04

Editorial director: Tina B. Carver
Senior sponsoring editor: Thomas Healy
Senior development editor: Arley Gray
Production manager: Juanita Thompson
Interior designer: Nesbitt Graphics, Inc.
Cover designer: Nesbitt Graphics, Inc.
Illustrators: Reggie Holladay, Bill Petersen
Photo research: Nesbitt Graphics, Inc.

ICON 1 Components

Student Book	0-07-255039-2
Workbook	0-07-255040-6
Teacher's Manual	0-07-255041-4
Audio Cassettes	0-07-255042-2
Audio CDs	0-07-255043-0

ICON Teaching-Learning Video   0-07-301662-4

International Edition   ISBN: 0-07-111725-3
Copyright © 2005. Exclusive rights by the McGraw-Hill Companies, Inc., for manufacture and export. This book cannot be re-exported from the country to which it is sold by McGraw-Hill. The International Edition is not available in North America.

Contents

1

A. Look at the pictures. Check (✓) the correct sentences.

1. ☐ I sometimes come to class late.
   ☐ I never come to class late.

3. ☐ I sometimes daydream in class.
   ☐ I never daydream in class.

2. ☐ I usually doodle in class.
   ☐ I never doodle in class.

4. ☐ I almost always look up new words.
   ☐ I never look up new words.

B. Complete the sentences. Use the words in the box.

ask	come	look up	write down

1. Do you usually _____ the homework assignment?

3. Do you ever _____ questions in class?

2. Do you ever _____ to class late?

4. Do you usually _____ every new word?

C. Complete the chart. Use the sentences in the box.

I usually write down the homework assignment.	I almost always forget my homework.	I always answer questions in class.
I sometimes get to class late.	I sometimes write e-mails in English.	I never watch movies in English.

Good ideas

_____

_____

_____

_____

Bad ideas

_____

_____

_____

_____

D. Write one good idea and one bad idea of your own in the chart above.

E. Complete the conversations. Use the words and phrases in the box.

chat online	doodle	practice	watch DVDs

1. A: Do you ever write e-mails in English?

   B: Yes, and I sometimes _____ in English, too. I have friends in England and Australia.

2. A: Do you ever write in your book?

   B: No, but I always _____ in my notebook.

3. A: Do you ever listen to CDs in English?

   B: No, but I sometimes _____ in English.

4. A: Do you ever speak English with your friends?

   B: No, never. But I sometimes _____ with my classmates.

2

A. Look at the chart. Complete the conversations. Use *ever, always, almost always, sometimes, hardly ever,* or *never.*

	Mon.	Tues.	Wed.	Thurs.	Fri.	Sat.	Sun.
1. speak your first language		X			X		X
2. chew gum							
3. forget your books			X				
4. listen to songs in English	X	X	X	X	X	X	X
5. do homework in the evening	X	X	X		X	X	X

1. Tom: Do you *ever speak your first language* ?

Sergio: Yes, I *sometimes speak my first language* .

2. Tom: Do you _____ ?

Sergio: No, I _____ .

3. Tom: Do you _____ ?

Sergio: No, I _____ .

4. Tom: Do you _____ ?

Sergio: Yes, I _____ .

5. Tom: Do you _____ ?

Sergio: Yes, I _____ .

B. Complete the sentences with *always, almost always, usually, sometimes, hardly ever,* or *never.* Use true information.

1. I _____ get to class on time.

2. I _____ take notes in class.

3. I _____ use new vocabulary words.

4. I _____ fall asleep in class.

5. I _____ listen to the teacher.

6. I _____ forget my books.

3

A. Complete the conversations. Use the sentences in the box.

Your mother?	Did you say page 15?	Did you say their shirts?
Good-bye?	Did you say 7:30?	Andy's?

1. Carlos: Do you like my ring? It's from
my brother.

Patty: _____

Carlos: No, my brother.

2. Maria: I usually study at Annie's house.

Joey: _____

Maria: No, Annie's.

3. Ali: Tuesday's homework assignment is
on page 15.

Kate: _____

Ali: Yeah, that's right.

4. Kim: I always shop at Candy's. I love
their skirts.

Bec: _____

Kim: No, their skirts. They have
beautiful skirts.

5. Pierre: I usually get to school around
6:30.

Lisa: _____

Pierre: No, 6:30. My class is at 7:00.

6. Ana: *Buenas noches* means "good
night" in Spanish.

Charlie: _____

Ana: No, good night.

B. Rewrite the conversations. Put the sentences in the correct order.

1. Did you say Room fourteen?
   Where's Room forty?
   No, forty.

   A: _____
   B: _____
   A: _____

2. No, it's not *my* birthday. It's Maya's!
   Well, happy birthday, Sarah!
   Today's Maya's birthday.

   A: _____
   B: _____
   A: _____

3. We saw a great movie on Sunday night.
   No, Sunday.
   Saturday night?

   A: _____
   B: _____
   A: _____

4. How often do I answer questions?
   How often do you ask questions in class?
   No, ask.

   A: _____
   B: _____
   A: _____

5. Yes, that's right.
   Ms. Bloom is our teacher this year.
   Did you say Ms. Bloom?

   A: _____
   B: _____
   A: _____

C. Think about confirming questions you might use. Write conversations like the ones above.

1. A: _____.
   B: _____?
   A: _____.

2. A: _____.
   B: _____?
   A: _____.

3. A: _____.
   B: _____?
   A: _____.

4

A. Read the tips. Take notes.

Homework Tips for Teachers

Most teachers give homework, but some students don't do it. Maybe the students just forget about it. Maybe they are too busy with other activities. Or maybe they are just too tired at the end of the day. One professor did some research. He has some suggestions for teachers:

- Don't give the assignment at the end of the class. Students will miss it because they are busy getting ready to leave.

- Be sure students understand the assignment. If they don't understand it, they probably won't do it.

- Give students a choice of assignments. Let them choose one they will enjoy doing.

- Always correct the homework at the beginning of the next class so students will know the right answers.

Why don't some students do homework?	What are some good homework habits for teachers?
_____	_____
_____	_____
_____	_____

B. Make notes on your ideas about homework habits.

Why don't some of your friends do homework?	How can your teachers make homework more useful or interesting?
_____	_____
_____	_____
_____	_____

C. Write about your homework ideas and suggestions for teachers. Use your notes.

_____

_____

_____

2 I never watch soap operas.

1

A. Look at the pictures. Complete the conversations. Use the words in the box.

| game shows | the news | soap operas | sports shows | talk shows |

1. A: Do you watch TV?

B: Yes. I like _____.

2. A: Do you watch the news?

B: No, but we love

_____.

3. A: I like _____ a lot.
I always learn something.

B: I like them, too. Sometimes the
questions are really hard.

4. A: Do you watch sitcoms?

B: No, but I sometimes watch

_____.

5. A: Do you like talk shows?

B: No, but I watch

_____ every

morning.

B. Complete the sentences. Use the words and phrases in the box.

once in a while	almost every day	never	once a week

1. Raquel almost never watches soap operas.

   She watches soap operas

   _____.

2. Larry watches a soccer game every Saturday afternoon.

   He watches a sports show

   _____.

3. Linda usually watches the 6:00 news.

   She watches the news

   _____.

4. Patrick hates TV.

   He _____

   watches TV.

C. Check (✓) the correct response.

1. A: I'm watching *Beepers*. It's great.
   B: ☐ What channel is it on?
      ☐ Channel 5.

2. A: Hey, Jim. What's happening?
   B: ☐ *The Bachelor*.
      ☐ Not much.

3. A: What's on?
   B: ☐ A very interesting talk show.
      ☐ On Channel 9.

4. A: Why do you like that show?
   B: ☐ Almost every day.
      ☐ It's funny.

D. Complete the sentences. Use true information.

1. Almost all of my friends watch

   _____.
      (name of show)

2. It is a _____.
        (kind of show)

3. They watch the show

   _____.
      (how often)

4. They think it's

   _____ show.
   (a good/an interesting/a fantastic)

2

A. Match the questions and answers.

_____ **1.** Why do some people hate soap operas?

_____ **2.** What station do you like best?

_____ **3.** How many sitcoms did you watch Friday night?

_____ **4.** When did you see that show?

_____ **5.** What kinds of shows do you like?

_____ **6.** When is _Jeopardy_ on?

a. Channel 7.

b. I like game shows and sports.

c. Three or four.

d. Because they're silly.

e. Every night at 7:00.

f. Last night at 9:00.

B. Look at the pictures. Complete the questions. Use _What, When, Why,_ or _How many._

1.
_____ games did you watch yesterday?

2.
_____ do you hate game shows?

3.
_____ does the show start?

4.
_____ station has the weather at 6:00?

3

A. Number the lines of the conversations.

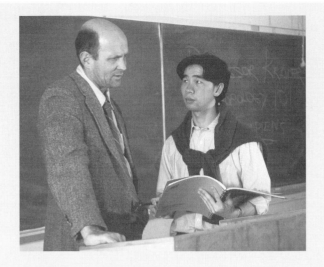

1. ____ Not every day, but often.

____ Hmmm. Well, I often watch at 6:00.

____ When do you watch the news on TV?

____ Every day?

3. ____ I watch *Make a Million* every week.

____ Right. That almost never happens.

____ Did you watch it last week?

____ Let me think. Oh, yes. The grandmother won $20,000 on that show.

2. ____ Yes, I do. I saw the story of Madonna's life last week.

____ Was it good?

____ Do you ever watch biographies on TV?

____ It was very interesting.

4. ____ Let me see. . . . A love story, I guess.

____ Oh, yeah? What kind of movie was it?

____ I watched a good movie on Channel 9 last night.

____ Oh, I like love stories!

B. Complete the conversations. Use the words and phrases in the box.

What's happening	Let me see	What's on	Not much	Regularly	Great	I guess

1. Barry: Let's watch TV.
   Lynn: _____?
   Barry: I don't know. Let's look in the newspaper.

2. Kim: What shows do you watch regularly?
   George: _____?
   Well, I watch my soap operas every day.
   Kim: Why do you watch soap operas?
   George: Because they're funny, _____.

3. Paco: Hi, Donna. _____?
   Donna: _____.
   Paco: Do you want to watch *Survivor*?
   Donna: Sure.

4. Sally: What's your favorite TV show?
   Bill: _____. . . .
   Well, I watch the news every evening.
   Sally: _____!
   Tell me what's happening in the world.

C. Complete the conversations. Use true information.

1. A friend: How many TV shows did you watch last night?
   You: _____

2. A friend: What's the name of a really good show?
   You: _____

3. Your teacher: Why do some people love sports shows?
   You: _____

4. A friend: _____
   You: Almost every day.
   A friend: Why do you watch it?
   You: _____

4

A. Read about soap operas. Take notes.

Soap Operas

Soap operas are over 50 years old. One of the first soap operas, *The Guiding Light,* is still on TV today. Soap operas got their name from the advertisers on the original shows. Most of these programs advertised soap and other household products that stay-at-home wives and mothers used. Today there are TV soap operas in almost every country in the world.

And today women aren't the only people who watch these dramas. Many men and women videotape the programs to watch when they get home from work. College students watch them between classes. Soap opera fans say the shows help them forget their problems. When they watch, they relax a little and laugh at life.

How old are soap operas? _____

What was one of the first soap operas? _____

Who watches soap operas? _____

Why are soap operas popular? _____

B. Make notes about your favorite TV show.

What is the name of your favorite show? _____

When did you first start watching it? _____

Why do you like this show? _____

Tell a little about last week's show. _____

C. Write about your favorite TV show. Use your notes.

_____

_____

_____

_____

3 We're going to take a day trip.

1

A. Complete the conversations. Use the words in the box.

fun	new	romantic	dangerous

1. A: What's a good place for a honeymoon?

   B: Niagara Falls. It's very _____.

2. A: Do you want to visit relatives on your next vacation?

   B: No, I don't. That's not _____.

3. A: Do you want to go surfing?

   B: No, I don't. Surfing is _____.

4. A: Do you want to go to the beach again?

   B: No, I don't. Let's go somewhere _____.

B. Look at the pictures. Check (✓) the correct sentences.

1. ☐ She wants to go sightseeing.
   ☐ She wants to go surfing.

2. ☐ He wants to visit relatives.
   ☐ He wants to go somewhere new.

3. ☐ She wants to visit relatives.
   ☐ She wants to go sightseeing.

4. ☐ She wants to hang out at the beach.
   ☐ She wants to go on a honeymoon.

C. Look at the pictures. Complete the sentences. Use a word from Box A and a phrase from Box B in each answer.

A	B
do	something fun
read	somewhere new
	something interesting
go	something dangerous

1. Teruyo is going to _____ _____.

2. Nina is going to _____ _____.

3. Lisa is going to _____ _____.

4. The Morgans are going to _____ _____.

D. List some vacation activities. Check (✓) your answer after each activity.

something interesting	_____	☐ I like this activity.	☐ I don't like this activity.
something exciting	_____	☐ I like this activity.	☐ I don't like this activity.
something relaxing	_____	☐ I like this activity.	☐ I don't like this activity.
something dangerous	_____	☐ I like this activity.	☐ I don't like this activity.

2

A. Unscramble the sentences. Begin each sentence with a capital letter.

1. _____

   (they / going to / what / tonight / are / do / ?)

2. _____

   (going to / this weekend / is / Mona / go somewhere new / .)

3. _____

   (we / on Sunday / going to / visit relatives / are / .)

4. _____

   (after class / do / are / going to / what / you / ?)

5. _____

   (he / is / what / do / going to / tonight / ?)

6. _____

   (stay home / I / going to / tomorrow / am / .)

B. Complete the conversations. Use *am, is, are, 'm not, isn't,* or *aren't.*

1. A: _____ you going to go
      sightseeing in Paris?

   B: No, I _____. I'm going to take
      a cooking class.

2. A: _____ David going to do
      something unusual this weekend?

   B: Yes, he _____. He's going to
      stay home!

3. A: _____ we going to do
      something fun after class?

   B: Yes, we _____. We're going to
      have a party.

4. A: _____ your sister going to visit
      you this summer?

   B: No, she _____. She's going to
      visit our parents.

3

A. Complete the conversations. Use the correct follow-up questions from the box.

Who are you going to go with?	How are you going to get there?
What are you going to do?	Where are you going to sleep?
When are you going to get here?	Where are you going to eat?

1. A: We're going to visit relatives in Centerville this weekend.

   B: _____

   A: We're going to take the train.

2. A: I'm going to go surfing this weekend.

   B: _____

   A: Oh, I don't know. Maybe Jan and Dean.

3. A: Lee and I are going to do something unusual.

   B: _____

   A: We're going to visit Alaska in the winter.

4. A: I'm going to visit my uncle Hal this weekend.

   B: _____

   A: In his living room.

5. A: I'm going to be late for class next Tuesday.

   B: _____

   A: Probably around 11:30.

6. A: I'm going to have dinner with my sister tonight.

   B: _____

   A: In a restaurant.

B. Complete the conversations. Use the questions and answers in the box.

Questions	Answers
are they going to get there?	They are going to go to the library.
are they going to stay?	They're going to try surfing.
are they going to go?	They are going to take the bus.
are they going to do?	They're going to be there a week.

1. A: Larry and Ellen are going to hang out at the beach this afternoon.

B: Really? How _____

A: _____

2. A: Bruce is going to study with Ellen tonight.

B: Where _____

A: _____

3. A: My parents are going to do something unusual.

B: What _____

A: _____

4. A: The soccer team is going to take a trip to Florida.

B: Really? How long _____

A: _____

C. Complete the conversation. Talk about what you are going to do on Saturday. Use true information.

A friend: Where _____

You: _____

A friend: How _____

You: _____

A friend: What _____

You: _____

4

A. Read about a vacation place. Take notes.

The Trip of a Lifetime

A visit to Southern California is the trip of a lifetime! You can relax and swim at one of the beautiful ocean beaches. Or you can try surfing. The studio tours in Hollywood are wonderful, too. The special effects are amazing. And it's really exciting to see a famous movie star up close. For real excitement and danger, there's always bungee-jumping. Imagine telling your friends about that when you get home! Southern California has it all.

Place: _____

Activity 1: _____ Description: _____

Activity 2: _____ Description: _____

Activity 3: _____ Description: _____

B. Make notes about another vacation place.

Place: _____

Activity 1: _____ Description: _____

Activity 2: _____ Description: _____

Activity 3: _____ Description: _____

C. Write about the place. Use your notes.

_____

_____

_____

_____

_____

4 I can't take your call . . .

1

A. Look at the pictures. Check (✓) the correct sentences.

Anna

Victor

Can you tell me when Matrix Six starts?

Shan-Lei

Fatima

1. ☐ She's checking the movie listings.
☐ She's checking the weather forecast.

3. ☐ He's checking a bus schedule.
☐ He's checking a movie listing.

2. ☐ She's checking a sports score.
☐ She's checking a movie listing.

4. ☐ She's checking a sports score.
☐ She's checking a bus schedule.

B. Look at the pictures above. Complete the sentences. Use the phrases in the box.

watches TV	looks in the newspaper	uses the phone	looks online

1. Anna _____ to get the information.

3. Victor _____ to get the information.

2. Shan-Lei _____ to get the information.

4. Fatima _____ to get the information.

C. Complete the conversations. Use the phrases in the box.

can leave a message	am returning your call
need directions to the theater	am about to go out
can't take your call right now	

1. A: Monica said you called this morning, so I
   _____. What's up?

   B: Do you want to go to a movie tonight?

2. A: Hi, Jackie. How are you?
   B: Fine, but I can't talk now. I _____.

3. A: Jerry isn't home right now.
   B: That's okay. I _____.

4. A: This is 343-8191. I _____. Please leave a
   message.

   B: This is Bruce. Please call me at 591-2228.

5. A: This is 343-1758. Please leave a message.
   B: I _____. I lost the address. Please call me
   back.

D. Write a voice mail message for your phone. Then write a message from a friend. Use true information.

Voice mail message:

_____

_____

_____

Friend's message:

_____

_____

_____

2

A. Complete the questions with *Where, How,* or *When* + *can*. Complete the answers with *can*.

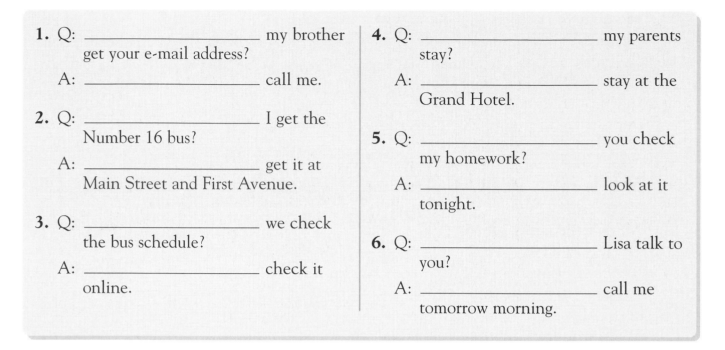

1. Q: _____ my brother get your e-mail address?

   A: _____ call me.

2. Q: _____ I get the Number 16 bus?

   A: _____ get it at Main Street and First Avenue.

3. Q: _____ we check the bus schedule?

   A: _____ check it online.

4. Q: _____ my parents stay?

   A: _____ stay at the Grand Hotel.

5. Q: _____ you check my homework?

   A: _____ look at it tonight.

6. Q: _____ Lisa talk to you?

   A: _____ call me tomorrow morning.

B. Rewrite the statements as questions. Complete the answers.

1. She can't take your call right now.

   Q: _____?

   A: No, _____.

2. We can't send it by e-mail.

   Q: _____?

   A: No, _____.

3. We can meet for lunch tomorrow.

   Q: _____?

   A: Yes, _____.

4. They can't get downtown from here.

   Q: _____?

   A: No, _____.

3

A. Number the lines of the conversations.

1. ____ Can you recommend a good one?

   ____ Do you ever hang out at the beach?

   ____ Yes, I do.

   ____ I like Gilgo Beach. You can surf there.

3. ____ How do you check the weather forecast?

   ____ Channcl 37.

   ____ What channel is that?

   ____ I watch the Weather Channel.

2. ____ I use cars dot com.

   ____ You can try the Internet.

   ____ I want to buy a new car.

   ____ Can you recommend a good website?

4. ____ You can look in the newspaper.

   ____ I want to find a cheap apartment. Can you recommend a way to find one?

   ____ The *Daily Record* has a lot of ads.

   ____ That's a good idea. What's a good newspaper?

B. Complete the conversations. Use the sentences in the box.

Can you recommend a good restaurant?	How can I learn new words?
What's a good website?	What's a good TV show for my daughter? She's six.
Do you know a good clothing store?	Can you recommend a music store?

1. Carl: _____

   Linda: There are some cute shows for children on Channel 13.

2. Isabel: I'm interested in jazz CDs. _____

   Bert: Try CD Heaven on Hamilton Avenue.

3. Harry: _____

   Sally: Sure. I usually eat at Mabel's. It's great!

4. Willy: I need to learn more about dogs. _____

   Ned: Try man'sbestfriend dot com.

5. Nilda: _____

   Alice: Yes, I do. Try Clothes Line on Fifth Avenue.

6. Oliver: I need to learn more English vocabulary. _____

   Jean: You can watch movies in English.

C. Complete the conversations. Use true information.

1. A friend: Can you recommend an interesting website?

   You: _____

2. A friend: What's a good place to buy cheap shoes?

   You: _____

3. A classmate: Can you recommend a good way to study for the next test?

   You: _____

4. A friend: How can I meet new people?

   You: _____

A. Read about cell phones. Take notes.

Cell Phones: Useful or Dangerous?

Today over 80 million people in the United States regularly use cell phones. They are useful in many ways. People on vacation can call from their cars to find a hotel. Drivers can call the police if they see an accident on the road. Parents can find out where their teenage children are at night. However, cell phones also cause problems. Drivers sometimes look at their cell phone instead of at the road. Or they may have an angry conversation and forget they are driving. Hundreds of accidents happen every year because of this.

What are some recommendations for cell phone safety? Memorize where the buttons are on your phone. Use the "hands free" feature so you don't have to hold the phone while you are talking. Never drive and use the phone when you are angry or upset. And if you can, pull over to the side of the road before making a call.

Advantages of cell phones: _____

_____

Problems with cell phones: _____

_____

Recommendations: _____

_____

B. Make notes about the advantages of and problems with another everyday item, such as televisions, personal CD players, or computers.

Advantages of _____ : _____

Problems with _____ : _____

Recommendations: _____

C. Write about the item you chose. Use your notes.

_____

_____

_____

1

A. Look at the pictures. Complete the sentences. Use the phrases in the box. More than one answer may be possible.

interesting work	a high salary	job security
a good boss	lots of time off	an easy commute

1. _____ is important to Mustafa.

2. Sally doesn't have _____.

3. Having _____ is important to Carlos.

4. Raquel has _____.

5. John has _____.

6. Lisa has _____.

B. Match the sentence parts.

_____ **1.** A high   **a.** commute.

_____ **2.** I have a very good   **b.** security.

_____ **3.** I want a lot of   **c.** salary is important to me.

_____ **4.** Pete has an easy   **d.** work.

_____ **5.** We don't have job   **e.** time off.

_____ **6.** I like interesting   **f.** boss.

C. Check (✓) three correct sentences for each picture.

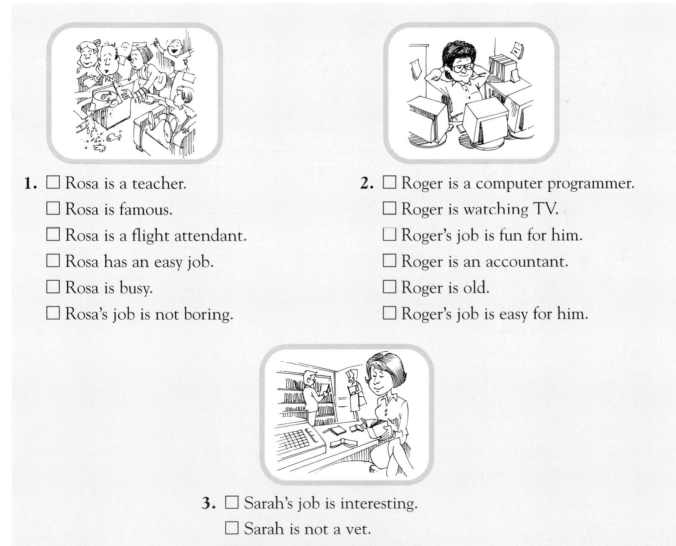

1. ☐ Rosa is a teacher.
    ☐ Rosa is famous.
    ☐ Rosa is a flight attendant.
    ☐ Rosa has an easy job.
    ☐ Rosa is busy.
    ☐ Rosa's job is not boring.

2. ☐ Roger is a computer programmer.
    ☐ Roger is watching TV.
    ☐ Roger's job is fun for him.
    ☐ Roger is an accountant.
    ☐ Roger is old.
    ☐ Roger's job is easy for him.

3. ☐ Sarah's job is interesting.
    ☐ Sarah is not a vet.
    ☐ Sarah is a travel agent.
    ☐ Sarah's job is dangerous.
    ☐ Sarah is always busy.
    ☐ Sarah is the owner of a bookstore.

2

A. Read about the people's jobs. Complete the sentences. Use the words in parentheses.

1. Jake and Linda work in a factory. Linda is Jake's boss. Her job is more difficult than Jake's. Linda works nine hours a day, but Jake works only seven hours. Jake's job is boring, but Linda's isn't.

   (long hours)   Linda works _____ Jake.

   (interesting)   Linda's job is _____ Jake's job.

   (easy)   Jake's job is _____ Linda's job.

2. Tim and Tina are good friends. Tim is a teacher. He doesn't earn a lot of money, but his life is hardly ever boring. Tina is a famous singer. She is on TV every week. She's rich, but she isn't happy. Her life is very stressful.

   (a good salary) Tina gets _____ Tim.

   (famous)   Tina is _____ Tim.

   (happy)   Tim is _____ Tina.

3. Marta works as a computer programmer. She is 33 years old, and her boss is 25. Marta's boss isn't very smart. This is very stressful for Marta. Marta's sister, Mary, works for a doctor. She has a great boss. He's a funny man, and Mary loves her job.

   (young)   Marta's boss is _____ Marta.

   (a bad boss)   Marta has _____ Mary.

   (stressful)   Marta's job is _____ Mary's.

4. Mark Madison is a rich man. He doesn't have a job. He plays tennis and golf all day. But he's not very happy. His friend Paul doesn't have a lot of money, but he loves his job. He's a vet. It's an exciting job.

   (rich)   Mark is _____ Paul.

   (happy)   Paul is _____ Mark.

   (exciting)   Paul's life is _____ Mark's.

B. Compare yourself with other people. Use true information.

1. (young)   My _____ is _____.

2. (interesting) My _____ is _____.

3. (good)   My _____ is _____.

3

A. Complete the conversations with sentences from the box.

I like animals better than people.	But it's dangerous work.	I'd rather be a firefighter.
I'd like to travel all the time.	I love money.	But traveling can be stressful.
But the salary is worse.	But everyone would know your name.	

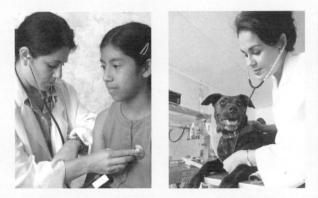

1. A: Would you rather be a doctor or a vet?

B: I'd rather be a vet.
_____

A: _____

B: I don't care about money. This kind of work is more interesting to me.

2. A: Would you rather be a computer programmer or a firefighter?

B: _____

A: _____

B: I'm not afraid. And it's important work.

3. A: Would you rather be rich or famous?

B: I'd rather be rich.
_____

A: _____

B: I don't care. I need the security.

4. A: Would you rather be a travel agent or a flight attendant?

B: I'd rather be a flight attendant.
_____

A: _____

B: But that's better than being bored.

B. Check (✓) the correct response.

1. A: How difficult is your job?
   B: ☐ It's a breeze. ☐ It's very important.

2. A: What would you rather be?
   B: ☐ A bookstore owner.
   ☐ An easy commute.

3. A: How important is a high salary to you?
   B: ☐ Not very. ☐ It's crazy.

4. A: I'd rather be a teacher. The work is fun.
   B: ☐ Yes, and you can work at home.
   ☐ Yes, and you have lots of time off.

5. A: What would you rather have?
   B: ☐ Job security. ☐ An architect.

6. A: He's a police officer, and she's a computer programmer.
   B: ☐ His job is more stressful.
   ☐ Her job is more dangerous.

C. Unscramble the sentences. Begin each sentence with a capital letter.

1. _____
   (security / have / job / we / good / .)

2. _____
   (a vet / an accountant / be / you / would / rather / or / ?)

3. _____
   (important / interesting / you / to / work / is / how / ?)

4. _____
   (very / a high / think / is / I / salary / important / .)

5. _____
   (a travel agent's job / more / than / a police officer's job / dangerous / is / .)

6. _____
   (an architect / think / gets / do / a good salary / you / ?)

4

A. Read about the people's jobs. Take notes.

I'm a glazier. My job involves cutting glass and installing large windows in supermarkets, auto dealerships, and banks. I also install glass doors, windows, and mirrors in people's homes. Once I even built a glass-top table. It's interesting work, and I have great job security because people are always breaking glass.

Name of job: _____

Information: _____

_____

I'm a library assistant. My job is to help the librarian. I take down information from new patrons and make up library cards. Then I enter the information in the computer. I also check out books and magazines and videotapes at the front desk and put returned books back on the shelves. Sometimes I send out e-mails to people who don't bring back their books on time. The salary isn't great, but I have a great boss.

Name of job: _____

Information: _____

_____

B. Make notes about a job you would like to have.

Name of job: _____

Responsibilities: _____

Advantages and disadvantages: _____

C. Write about the job you chose. Use your notes.

_____

_____

_____

6 She's really outgoing!

1

A. Complete the sentences. Use the words in the box.

messy	funny	neat	outgoing	serious	quiet	lazy	hardworking

1. Luis is _____.

He isn't _____.

2. The room is _____.

It isn't _____.

3. Megan is _____.

She isn't _____.

4. The TV program is _____.

It isn't _____.

B. Complete the sentences. Use the words in the box.

hardworking	funny	lazy	outgoing

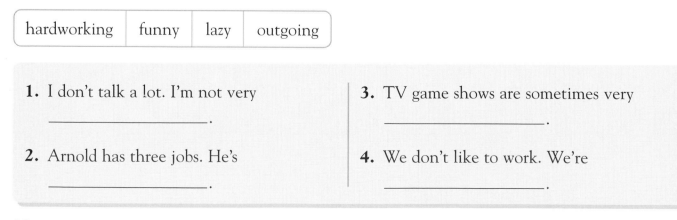

1. I don't talk a lot. I'm not very

_____.

2. Arnold has three jobs. He's

_____.

3. TV game shows are sometimes very

_____.

4. We don't like to work. We're

_____.

C. Look at the pictures. Check (✓) the correct sentences.

Cesar 17, Delia 14, Vidal 10

Jacob 11

Elvira 17, Alisa 14

1. ☐ Cesar is the middle child.
   ☐ Cesar is the oldest child.

2. ☐ Alisa is younger than Elvira.
   ☐ Alisa is an only child.

3. ☐ Delia is younger than Vidal.
   ☐ Delia is the middle child.

4. ☐ Jacob is an only child.
   ☐ Jacob is the youngest child.

5. ☐ Elvira is younger than Alisa.
   ☐ Elvira is older than Alisa.

6. ☐ Vidal is an only child.
   ☐ Vidal is the youngest child.

D. List your favorite movie and TV stars. Write one or two personal characteristics of each person.

Name	Personal characteristics

2

A. Complete the conversations. Use the words in parentheses.

1. (old)   Tina: Are you _____ than your brother?

    (old)   Yolanda: Yes, I am. I am _____ child in my family.

2. (good)   David: Are you a _____ swimmer than your sister?

    (good)   Andy: No, she's _____ swimmer in my family.

3. (funny)   Rhona: Are you _____ child in your family?

    (funny)   Dick: No, my brother is _____ than me.

4. (athletic) Mike: Who's _____ person in your family?

    (athletic) Luis: My father is. He's _____ than me.

5. (serious)   Ping: Are you _____ student in your class?

    (relaxed)   Kham: No, I'm _____ student.

6. (neat)   Ben: Who is _____ person in your family?

    (messy)   Cara: Not me! I'm _____ of all.

B. Complete the sentences. Use true information.

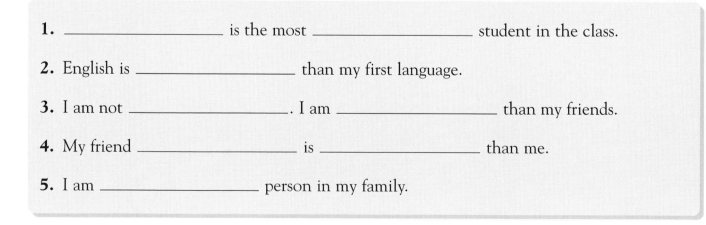

1. _____ is the most _____ student in the class.

2. English is _____ than my first language.

3. I am not _____. I am _____ than my friends.

4. My friend _____ is _____ than me.

5. I am _____ person in my family.

3

A. Write conversations. Use the sentences in the boxes.

> Oh, yeah? What does he do?
>
> He works 40 hours a week and goes to school at night.
>
> Jorge is a hardworking guy.

1. A: _____

B: _____

_____

A: _____

> I have a problem.
>
> I study hard, but I don't get good grades.
>
> Is that so? What is it?

2. A: _____

B: _____

_____

A: _____

_____

> I see. What's the problem?
>
> I'm going to visit a sick relative.
>
> I'm not going to be in class tomorrow.

3. A: _____

B: _____

_____

A: _____

_____

B. Check (✓) the correct response.

1. A: Who's the tallest person in your class?
   B: Gregory. He's a basketball player.
   A: ☐ He's very tall. ☐ Is that so?
   B: Yes. He's the best player on the team.
   A: ☐ Really? That's great. ☐ You are?

2. A: What does your sister do?
   B: She's a travel agent.
   A: ☐ I see.
      ☐ Really? Where does she work?
   B: In New York City.
   A: ☐ Oh, yeah?
      ☐ I see. That's an exciting place to work.

3. A: The Olsens are a funny family.
   B: Really? Who's the funniest person in the family?
   A: ☐ Mr. Olsen. He's a riot.
      ☐ Tony. He's very rude.
   B: Is that so?
   A: ☐ Yes, I agree.
      ☐ Yes, he's a lot of fun.

4. A: What do you do on weekends?
   B: I run and play baseball.
   A: ☐ Is that so? Do you play on a team?
      ☐ I see.
   B: Yes. We play in Andreas Park.
   A: ☐ Really? Who is that?
      ☐ Oh, yeah? That's near my house.

5. A: Who's the oldest person in your family?
   B: My grandfather, I guess.
   A: ☐ I see. ☐ Really? How old is he?
   B: He's 95 years old.
   A: ☐ Is that so? That's pretty old!
      ☐ I see. He's quiet.

C. Write the conversation. Use the sentences in the box.

No, he's just lazy.	Is he very relaxed?
Really?	My brother.
Who is the messiest person you know?	

Roger: _____
Anna: _____

Roger: _____
Anna: _____

4

A. Read about personality types.

Are You a Type A or a Type B?

Scientists divide humans into two basic personality types—Type A and Type B. Type A people are always in a hurry. They often do two things at the same time. They read the newspaper or watch TV while they eat. They read their mail while talking on the telephone. Type A personalities often become angry at other drivers, and they don't like to wait in line. Many Type A people don't sleep well at night, and they also get sick more often than Type B people.

The Type B personality is the opposite. Type B people are relaxed about everything. They enjoy life and take it one day at a time. They are hardly ever in a hurry. They don't always get good grades in school, and they often make less money than their Type A friends. Some people call them lazy, but they call themselves relaxed. They are pretty happy with life and usually live longer than Type A people.

B. Are you a Type A or a Type B person? List ideas and facts about yourself to prove it.

Choose one: ☐ I am a Type A person. ☐ I am a Type B person.

_____

_____

_____

_____

C. Write about your personality. Use your notes.

_____

_____

_____

_____

_____

1

A. Look at the pictures. Complete the sentences. Use a word from Box A and a word from Box B in each answer.

A	semester	science	art	literature	Spanish	math
B	calculus	sculpture	history	chemistry	language	Russian

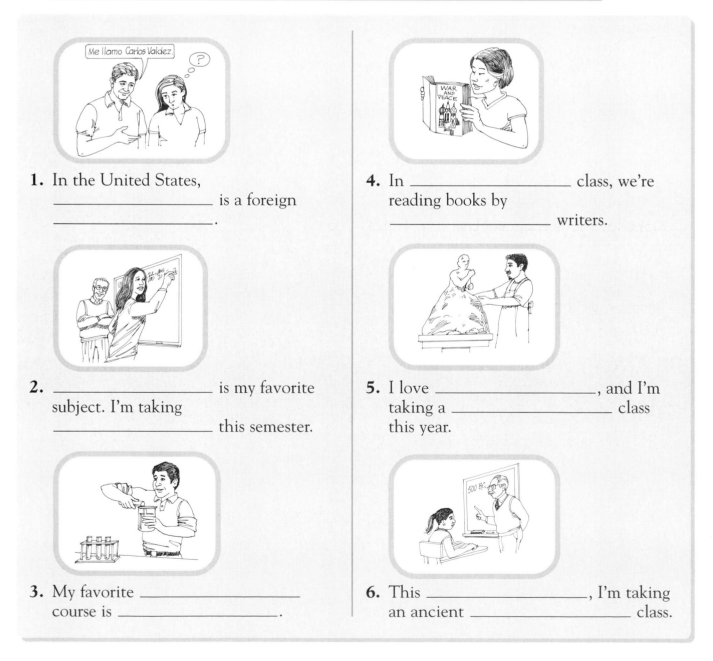

1. In the United States, _____ is a foreign _____.

2. _____ is my favorite subject. I'm taking _____ this semester.

3. My favorite _____ course is _____.

4. In _____ class, we're reading books by _____ writers.

5. I love _____, and I'm taking a _____ class this year.

6. This _____, I'm taking an ancient _____ class.

B. Check (✓) the word that means the same as the first one.

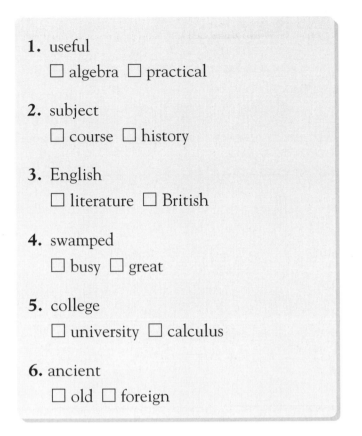

1. useful
   ☐ algebra ☐ practical

2. subject
   ☐ course ☐ history

3. English
   ☐ literature ☐ British

4. swamped
   ☐ busy ☐ great

5. college
   ☐ university ☐ calculus

6. ancient
   ☐ old ☐ foreign

C. Complete the sentences. Use true information.

1. I think _____ is an interesting subject.

2. I don't/didn't like _____ class.

3. My favorite _____ class is/was _____.

4. No one in my family took _____ in school.

5. Everyone should study _____.

6. I don't think _____ is useful.

2

A. Complete the sentences. Use *should* or *shouldn't*.

1. The man _____ carry so many boxes.

2. The woman _____ help the man.

3. The boy _____ stop the dog.

B. Complete the sentences. Use *have to* or *don't have to*.

1. The girls _____ pay $6.00.

2. The women _____ pay.

3. The men _____ pay $10.00.

C. Rewrite the statements. Use *should, shouldn't, have to,* or *don't have to*.

1. It's necessary for students to take a final exam in this course.

   Students _____
   _____

2. It's a good idea for students to study every night.

   Students _____
   _____

3. It's a bad idea for students to be late to class.

   Students _____
   _____

4. It's not necessary for students to study in the library.

   Students _____
   _____

5. It isn't useful for students to look up every word in the dictionary.

   Students _____
   _____

6. It's necessary for students to bring their books to class every day.

   Students _____
   _____

3

A. Complete the conversations with sentences from the box.

I feel strongly that everyone should play soccer.	I think it would be fun to be a flight attendant.
In my opinion, science is more difficult.	I don't think small children should use computers.
Oh, I don't think it's so hard.	I don't think a few hours a week is a problem.
In my opinion, people should choose a job they like.	I think people should choose their own sport.

1. A: Math is really difficult.

B: _____

_____

A: You don't?

B: No. _____

_____

2. A: _____

_____

B: Why do you say that?

A: Well, exercise is really important for everyone.

B: Yeah, but _____

_____

3. A: _____

_____

B: Why not?

A: Because they should be playing outside.

A: Well, _____

_____

4. A: What job do you dream about doing?

B: _____

_____

A: Really?

B: Yeah. _____

_____

B. Number the lines of the conversations.

1. ____ In my opinion, expensive cars are a waste of money.

   ____ I don't think people should buy expensive cars.

   ____ Why not?

   ____ My brother just bought a fancy sports car.

2. ____ Do you watch the news on TV every day?

   ____ Well, sometimes I read the newspaper.

   ____ No, I don't. I think it's boring.

   ____ I feel strongly that everyone should know what's happening.

3. ____ Why not?

   ____ I think everyone should see *Maximum Force*.

   ____ In my opinion, it's an awful movie.

   ____ Well, I don't.

C. Write a conversation expressing opinions. Use true information.

A friend: In my opinion, _____

You: I don't agree. _____

A friend: _____

You: _____

A friend: _____

You: _____

4

A. Read about distance learning. Take notes.

Distance Learning

Many people think they can't get a college education because they are too busy. They have jobs and family responsibilities that take up a lot of time. But now there is a way they can complete college without quitting their jobs or spending a lot of time away from their families. It's called distance learning. With distance-learning programs, college students can take courses off campus using printed materials, CD-ROMs, videotapes, cable TV, and Internet-based instruction.

Distance-learning programs give students all the things they need to get started— textbooks, CD-ROMs, etc. Everything is delivered to the student's house in one big box. Some schools offer programs that can be completed using a home computer with an Internet hookup that connects the student to the educational institution. Some programs have a satellite TV hookup that allows the at-home student to watch actual classes in session. Most such programs also have an interactive component that allows students to participate in discussions and ask the teacher questions from home. If you want to get a college education without leaving home, distance learning may be your answer.

Why some people don't go to college: _____

Advantages of distance learning: _____

How students learn using distance learning: _____

_____

B. Make notes about a distance-learning course you would like to take.

Name of course: _____

What you want to learn: _____

How this distance-learning course might work: _____

_____

C. Write about the course. Use your notes.

_____

_____

_____

8 It's easy come, easy go.

1

A. Check (✓) two correct sentences for each picture.

1. ☐ Alan is cheap.
☐ Alan is a spender.
☐ Alan is spending money on clothes.
☐ Alan is putting money in the bank.

3. ☐ Bruce is spending money.
☐ Bruce is putting money in the bank.
☐ Bruce is saving money.
☐ Bruce isn't using a credit card.

2. ☐ Clara is buying a gift.
☐ Clara is broke.
☐ Clara is using a credit card.
☐ Clara is cheap.

4. ☐ Pedro is a saver.
☐ Pedro is using a credit card.
☐ Pedro is putting money in the bank.
☐ Pedro is spending money.

B. Complete the sentences. Use the words in the box.

| department | drop | need | save | come | gift | broke | spender |

1. Did you ever buy something you didn't really _____?

2. Are you a _____ or a saver?

3. Tomorrow is Suzy's birthday. I need to buy a _____.

4. Do you often buy things in a _____ store?

5. Oh, well. It's easy _____, easy go.

6. I love to spend money, so I'm often _____.

7. I never shop until I _____.

8. I love to _____ money!

C. Complete the sentences about your spending habits. Use true information.

1. I always _____.

2. I sometimes _____.

3. I never _____.

4. I usually _____.

5. If I need money, I _____.

2

A. Unscramble the questions. Begin each sentence with a capital letter.

1. to save money / it's important / do you think

   _____

   _____

2. do you think / or credit cards / it's easier / to use cash

   _____

   _____

3. it's smart / to borrow money / do you think

   _____

   _____

4. to buy something you don't need / do you think / it's foolish

   _____

   _____

B. Rewrite the statements as questions. Start with the words *Do you think* . . . . Complete the answers.

1. It's foolish to borrow money.

   Q: _____

   _____?

   A: Yes, _____.

2. It's better to use credit cards than to use cash.

   Q: _____

   _____?

   A: It's _____ to use cash.

3. It's easy to earn money.

   Q: _____

   _____?

   A: No, _____.

4. It's smart to save money.

   Q: _____

   _____?

   A: Yes, _____.

5. It's harder to earn money than to save it.

   Q: _____

   _____?

   A: It's _____ to save it.

6. It's more important to give money to charity than to save it.

   Q: _____

   _____?

   A: It's more important _____ money to charity.

3

A. Write conversations. Use the sentences in the boxes.

That makes sense to me.	I'm tired. I want to take a nap.
The weather is great. I'd rather go swimming.	Why don't we go swimming and then take a nap?

1. A: _____
   B: _____
   A: _____
   B: _____

Then let's go!	Actually, I'd rather take a helicopter ride.
Oh, I like that idea because I want to see the whole island.	Let's go sailing.

2. A: _____
   B: _____
   A: _____
   B: _____

But do you think it's good for the children?	Sure. I enjoy it.
Do you think it's okay to have the TV on all evening?	Maybe not. Why don't we turn it off at 7:00?

3. A: _____
   B: _____
   A: _____
   B: _____

B. Check (✓) the correct response.

1. A: Let's take a French course next semester.
   B: ☐ Why don't we study French?
   ☐ I like that idea because I love learning languages.

2. A: I have a big math test on Friday, so I'm going to study a little tonight and a little tomorrow night. What do you think?
   B: ☐ That makes sense to me.
   ☐ I like that idea because I'm tired.

3. A: We should take a math course.
   B: ☐ Why don't we take calculus?
   ☐ That makes sense to me. Let's take Greek.

4. A: Let's borrow some money and buy a new car.
   B: ☐ Why don't we take the money out of the bank?
   ☐ I'd rather buy a new car.

5. A: You should spend your birthday money on a new suit.
   B: ☐ I'd rather buy clothing.
   ☐ That makes sense to me.

C. Write a conversation where two people reach a compromise. Use at least two of these expressions: *I like that idea because . . . , That makes sense to me, Why don't we . . . , I'd rather . . . .*

A: _____

B: _____

A: _____

B: _____

4

A. Read about attitudes about money. Make notes about your family's attitudes about money.

My Money? Your Money? Our Money?

Many couples discover early in a relationship that they have very different attitudes about money. Some people are spenders and some are savers. If you want to understand where your attitudes come from, look back at your childhood. Did your parents use money as a reward or a punishment? Did your parents argue about money a lot? Was the family always worried about not having enough money? When both partners understand their own attitudes about money, they can begin to talk about how to spend and save their shared money with fewer problems.

One good way for couples to avoid fights is to decide together on the largest amount of money one person can spend without checking with the other person. That amount might be $50 or $100. Another technique is to plan purchases together ahead of time. Such a discussion might end with one person agreeing to spend $200 or less on a pair of skis, while the other person agrees to spend $200 or less on a new coat. A final point to remember is that it's important to return to the money topic often. This helps couples deal with money problems before they get too big.

Money as reward/punishment? _____

Arguments about money? _____

Not enough money? _____

Who was a spender/a saver? _____

Other? _____

B. Write about your attitudes about money. Explain how you (plan to) deal with money with your life partner.

_____

_____

_____

_____

9 Did you hit it off?

1

A. Complete the conversations. Use the phrases in the box.

the same level	the same taste	the same interests
the same amount	in common	hit it off

1. A: Did you have a good time?

B: Yeah. We have a lot _____.

We both love ice cream.

2. A: I'm sorry we can't agree on a film to rent.

B: Me, too. I guess we just don't have _____ in movies.

3. A: Did you _____ with your new roommate?

B: No. We don't like each other.

4. A: Do you and your sister have _____ of education?

B: No, we don't. My sister's a college professor.

5. A: Do you and your wife earn _____ of money?

B: Yes, we do. We teach in the same school.

6. A: Do you and your brother have _____?

B: No, we don't. He likes music, and I like sports. I like TV, and he likes reading.

B. Read each conversation. Check (✓) the answer that is true based on the conversation.

1. Jim: Hey, David. What do you want to do this afternoon?

   David: Let's go to that new movie, *Killer Bees*. Or we could go to the beach.

   Jim: No. I don't want to see that movie, and I don't like swimming.

   Jim and David ☐ have a lot in common.
                  ☐ have different interests.
                  ☐ really hit it off.

2. John: Let's go to a jazz club tonight.

   Lisa: Great idea. Nolan Rider is playing at the Hotspot.

   John: And then we can go for Indian food.

   Lisa: I'd rather have Chinese or Korean food.

   John and Lisa ☐ have the same taste in music.
                  ☐ have the same level of education.
                  ☐ have the same taste in food.

3. Linda: Let's move out of the dorm.

   Mei Young: Great idea! We can get a big two-bedroom apartment.

   Linda: Well, I don't know. That's probably too expensive for me.

   Linda and Mei Young ☐ don't have a lot in common.
                       ☐ don't have the same amount of money.
                       ☐ don't have the same religion.

4. Mike: They said on the news the hospital really needs type A blood.

   Jackie: That means they don't need me.

   Mike: Well, I'll be right back. I'm going to go give blood.

   Mike and Jackie ☐ didn't hit it off.
                    ☐ have different blood types.
                    ☐ are on a date.

A. Complete the conversations. Use the sentences in the box.

| Neither do I. | So am I. | So does Jim. | Neither does Jim. | So do I. | Neither am I. |

1. FACT: Jim always looks up new words
      in the dictionary.
   Classmate: I always look up new words
      in the dictionary.
   You: _____

2. FACT: You never ask questions in class.
   Classmate: Mary never asks questions in
      class.
   You: _____

3. FACT: Jim doesn't like tennis.
   Classmate: My friends don't like tennis.
   You: _____

4. FACT: You are a little messy.
   Classmate: I'm not very neat.
   You: _____

5. FACT: You love game shows on TV.
   Classmate: I really love game shows.
   You: _____

6. FACT: You are an outgoing person.
   Classmate: Larry is really outgoing.
   You: _____

B. Read B's *so* or *neither* response. Then choose the correct statement for A.

1. A: ☐ Roger isn't hardworking.
      ☐ Roger doesn't work hard.
   B: Neither am I.

2. A: ☐ I love Chinese food.
      ☐ I am hungry.
   B: So do I.

3. A: ☐ Tina tells funny jokes.
      ☐ Tina is really funny.
   B: So are you.

4. A: ☐ I don't exercise very much.
      ☐ I'm not an athlete.
   B: Neither is Carlos.

5. A: ☐ I'm not a very hardworking
      person.
      ☐ I don't study a lot.
   B: Neither does my roommate.

6. A: ☐ Frank is often late to class.
      ☐ Frank often comes to class late.
   B: So are we.

3

A. Complete the conversations with sentences from the box. More than one answer is possible.

| Good to talk to you. | Well, I have to go. | Nice talking to you. |

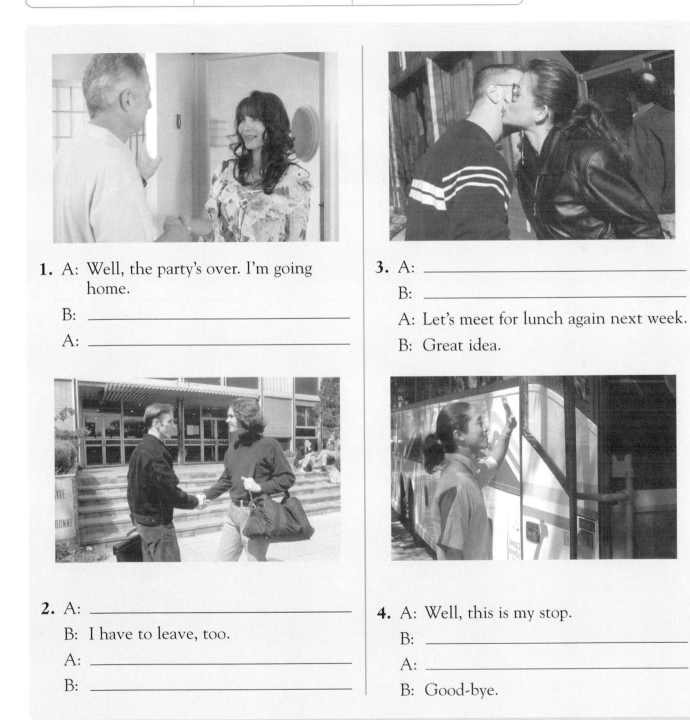

1. A: Well, the party's over. I'm going home.

B: _____

A: _____

2. A: _____

B: I have to leave, too.

A: _____

B: _____

3. A: _____

B: _____

A: Let's meet for lunch again next week.

B: Great idea.

4. A: Well, this is my stop.

B: _____

A: _____

B: Good-bye.

B. Here are the ends of three conversations. Number the lines.

1. ____ No, I really have to go.
   ____ OK. Nice talking to you.
   ____ Well, I have to go.
   ____ Can't you stay a few more minutes?

2. ____ Well, it was nice talking to you.
   ____ Yes, it is.
   ____ We have to go to class now.
   ____ Is it 4:00 already?

3. ____ Well, I have to go now.
   ____ Good-bye.
   ____ Nice talking to you, too.
   ____ Good to talk to you.

C. Read the conversation. Write an ending.

Mindy: So I hope you have a good time in Puerto Rico.

Sam: Thanks. I'm really excited about the trip.

Mindy: When are you going to leave?

Sam: _____

Mindy: _____

Sam: _____

Mindy: _____

Sam: _____

4

A. Read the article. List the steps in speed dating.

Speed Dating

Speed dating is just what it sounds like. It's a way of having a lot of dates in a short amount of time—a *very* short amount of time. Most speed dates last about six minutes.

The speed date leader invites a group of 20 or more men and women to meet in a public place, such as a club. The room is filled with tables for two people. Each person receives a number. The leader directs pairs to sit at each of the tables and start talking to each other. They have six minutes to find out what the other person is like. At the end of that time, the leader rings a bell. Conversation stops, and each person checks *Yes* or *No* on their "dating card" next to the number of the person they just met. Then everyone changes tables and meets another date. This continues until all the men and women meet each other.

At the end of the evening, everyone hands in their dating cards. The leader studies the results and sends out e-mail messages to the speed daters. The e-mail contains the name and the e-mail address or phone number of each person who checked *Yes* on their dating card after meeting the person. The speed daters can then contact each other and arrange a real date.

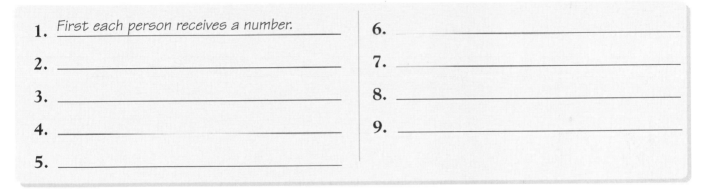

1. *First each person receives a number.*

2. _____

3. _____

4. _____

5. _____

6. _____

7. _____

8. _____

9. _____

B. What do you think of speed dating? What are the advantages? What are the disadvantages? Would you try it? Why or why not? Write your ideas.

10 I'd rather rough it.

1

A. Look at the pictures. Check (✓) the correct sentences.

1. ☐ Gina traveled with someone.
   ☐ Gina took the wrong train.

3. ☐ Patty stayed in a fancy hotel.
   ☐ Patty traveled light.

2. ☐ Carlos is taking a tour.
   ☐ Carlos is riding a camel.

4. ☐ Mehmet likes to rough it.
   ☐ Mehmet likes to skate.

B. Complete the sentences. Use the words and phrases in the box.

travel alone	travel light	uncomfortable	travel with everything	travel with someone

1. I usually have two or three suitcases.
   I like to _____ I might need.

2. Emily doesn't like to be alone.
   She likes to _____.

3. John wants to stay in fancy hotels. He doesn't like to be _____.

4. Lee doesn't like to go on group tours.
   He likes to _____.

5. Alice carries only her backpack when she travels. She likes to _____.

C. Complete the sentences. Use a phrase from column A and a word or phrase from column B in each answer.

A	B
in a fancy hotel	it
a camel	relaxed
with everything	a train
uncomfortable	a tour
your own trip	light

1. Would you rather ride _____ or ride _____?

2. Would you rather plan _____ or take _____?

3. Would you rather stay _____ or rough _____?

4. Would you rather travel _____ or travel _____?

5. Would you rather be _____ or be _____?

D. Write about your travel preferences.

1. I don't like to _____.

2. I prefer to _____.

3. I always _____.

4. Someday I would like to _____.

5. I never want to _____.

2

Look at each picture.
- Ask a general question using the present perfect.
- Give a short answer using the present perfect.
- For "yes" answers, add follow-up information in the past tense.
- Use the words in parentheses.

1. Question: (you, ever go, on a cruise)   Have you ever gone on a cruise?

    Answer: (yes)   Yes, I have.

    Follow-up: (go to Haiti last year)   I went to Haiti last year.

2. Question: (you, ever take, a tour)   _____

    Answer: (yes)   _____

    Follow-up: (take a tour of Italy in 2002)

3. Question: (you, ever fly, on a plane)   _____

    Answer: (yes)   _____

    Follow-up: (fly to Buenos Aires last month)   _____

4. Question: (you, ever lose, something)   _____

    Answer: (yes)   _____

    Follow-up: (lose my wallet this morning)   _____

3

A. Write conversations. Match the questions with the answers.

Follow-Up Questions	Answers
1. Where did you stay?	Yes, we did.
2. Who did you meet?	At noon.
3. Did you have fun?	My friend Abby.
4. When did you arrive?	We took an unusual tour.
5. What happened next?	At a fancy hotel.

1. Q: _____
A: _____

2. Q: _____
A: _____

3. Q: _____
A: _____

4. Q: _____
A: _____

5. Q: _____
A: _____

B. Check (✓) the correct follow-up question.

1. A: My wife is a model.
B: ☐ And has she ever been on TV?
☐ And does she ever travel?
A: Yes. She's been to Europe several times.

2. A: Amy went to India last year.
B: ☐ What did she visit?
☐ Who did she visit?
A: She saw the Taj Mahal.

3. A: I went bungee-jumping last weekend.
B: ☐ That's relaxing.
☐ That's dangerous.
A: You're right. I was really scared.

4. A: I stayed at a really fancy hotel.
B: ☐ Where was it?
☐ How long was it?
A: It was on Fifth Avenue.

5. A: I visited Los Angeles last month.
B: ☐ That sounds interesting.
☐ What did you do?
A: Yeah. I loved it.

6. A: We went to a classical music concert last night.
B: ☐ How was it?
☐ When was it?
A: It was wonderful.

C. Complete the conversations. Use the words in parentheses.

1. A:
   B: (yes)
   A: (what)
   B: (the Empire State Building)

    A: Have you ever been to New York City?
    B: _____
    A: _____
    B: _____

2. A:
   B: (yes)
   A: (who)
   B: (my family)

    A: Have you ever traveled with someone?
    B: _____
    A: _____
    B: _____

3. A:
   B: (yes)
   A: (what)
   B: (my watch)

    A: Have you ever lost something?
    B: _____
    A: _____
    B: _____

D. Complete the conversation. Talk about a movie you have seen. Use follow-up questions. Use true information.

You: _____

A friend: Who _____

You: _____

A friend: How _____

You: _____

4

A. Read the article. Take notes.

Electronic Check-In

Thanks to the Internet, it is often possible for travelers to check in for their flights before they leave for the airport. Electronic check-in allows travelers to avoid the long lines at the airport and can save a lot of time. If you choose this option, you can print out a boarding pass at home, instead of picking it up at the airport. You can confirm (or change) your seat assignment at any time. Some airlines also offer extra frequent-flyer miles if you check in electronically.

Electronic check-in is not for everyone, however. You can only use it if you are planning to carry all your luggage on the plane with you. If you plan to check any bags, you'll have to go through the regular check-in lines at the airport. Also, electronic check-in is only for flights within the U.S. If you're going to another country, you'll need to check in at the airport.

Advantages of electronic check-in	Problems with electronic check-in
_____	_____
_____	_____

B. Make notes about the advantages of and problems with another form of travel—for example, train travel, renting a car, or riding a bicycle.

Advantages of _____	Problems with _____
_____	_____
_____	_____

C. Write about the form of travel you chose. Use your notes.

_____

_____

_____

_____

_____

11 Are you stressed out?

1

A. Complete the conversations. Use the words and phrases in the box.

at the gym	to music	trouble sleeping	angry
a hot bath	meditate	stressed out	for a long walk

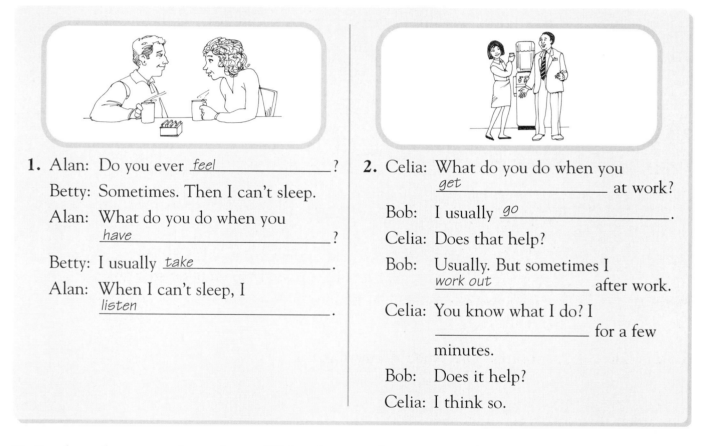

1. Alan: Do you ever _feel_____?

   Betty: Sometimes. Then I can't sleep.

   Alan: What do you do when you
   _have_____?

   Betty: I usually _take_____.

   Alan: When I can't sleep, I
   _listen_____.

2. Celia: What do you do when you
   _get_____ at work?

   Bob: I usually _go_____.

   Celia: Does that help?

   Bob: Usually. But sometimes I
   _work out_____ after work.

   Celia: You know what I do? I
   _____ for a few
   minutes.

   Bob: Does it help?

   Celia: I think so.

B. Look at the expressions above. Write them in the correct column.

Signs of Stress	Remedies
_____	_____
_____	_____
	_____
	_____

C. Check (✓) two correct sentences for each picture.

1. ☐ Nina is taking it easy.
   ☐ Nina is getting a massage.
   ☐ Nina is hardworking.
   ☐ Nina is taking a nap.

2. ☐ Matt has a headache.
   ☐ Matt is working out.
   ☐ Matt is taking a hot bath.
   ☐ Matt is angry.

3. ☐ Ellen feels angry.
   ☐ Ellen is having trouble concentrating in class.
   ☐ Ellen has a backache.
   ☐ Ellen has an upset stomach.

D. Complete the sentences. Use true information.

1. When I feel angry, I _____.

2. When I have a headache, I _____.

3. When my friends feel stressed out, they _____.

4. When I want to take it easy, I _____.

5. When I have trouble sleeping, I _____.

2

A. Look at the pictures. Complete the conversations.

1. Q: What do you do when _____ ?
   A: I _____ when _____ .

2. Q: What do you do when _____ ?
   A: I _____ when _____ .

3. Q: What do you do when _____ ?
   A: I _____ when _____ .

4. Q: What do you do when _____ ?
   A: I _____ when _____ .

B. Read the statements. Write questions and answers with *when*.

1. I drink coffee when I have trouble concentrating.
   Q: *When do you drink coffee?*
   A: *When I have trouble concentrating.*

2. I take a nap when I feel sleepy.
   Q: _____
   A: _____

3. I try to relax when I have to give a speech.
   Q: _____
   A: _____

4. I drink a lot of water when I have a cold.
   Q: _____
   A: _____

3

A. Number the lines of the conversations.

1. —— When do you hang out at the beach?
   —— Of course.
   —— When I don't have any work to do.
   —— Excuse me. Could I ask you a question?

2. —— Go right ahead.
   —— No, never.
   —— May I ask you a question?
   —— Do you ever fall asleep in class?

3. —— When I buy gifts for my family.
   —— May I ask you a question?
   —— When do you use your credit card?
   —— Okay. Go ahead.

4. —— On the Internet.
   —— Sure.
   —— Can I ask you something?
   —— Where do you buy your clothes?

5. —— When I have to give a speech.
   —— Excuse me. Could I ask you a question?
   —— When do you feel stressed out?
   —— Yes, you can.

B. Complete the conversations. Use the sentences in the box.

When do you get nervous?	Do you ever watch sports on TV?
Go right ahead.	Excuse me, miss. May I ask you a question?
Excuse me. Can I ask you a question?	When I have to take an exam.

1. Marta: _____

    Bill: Sure.

    Marta: _____

    Bill: No, but I like sitcoms.

2. Kim: Can I ask you something?

    Gary: Okay.

    Kim: _____

    Gary: _____

3. Tim: _____

    Linda: _____

    Tim: Where can I get the airport bus?

    Linda: It stops right there in front of the hotel.

C. Complete the conversations. Use true information.

1. A new student: Can I ask you a question?

    You: _____.

    A new student: Where can I buy a sandwich?

    You: _____.

2. A friend: May I ask you a question?

    You: _____.

    A friend: When do you get stressed out?

    You: _____.

3. You: _____

    Your teacher: Go right ahead.

    You: _____

    Your teacher: _____

4

A. Read the article. Follow the directions.

Handling Stress

Everyone's life has stress. There is no way to avoid it completely. But when we are aware of what causes stress, we can often handle it better. Sometimes we can plan our lives so that several stressful situations don't happen at the same time. Read the list of stressful situations below. Check (✓) the ones you have experienced in the last 12 months.

	Points		Points
☐ Death of husband or wife	100	☐ Changing type of work	35
☐ Death of a family member	60	☐ Making less money	40
☐ Death of a friend	40	☐ Change in work hours	20
☐ Getting married	50	☐ Having a child leave home	30
☐ Having a baby	40	☐ Beginning school	25
☐ Getting divorced	70	☐ Moving to a new city	25
☐ Being injured or sick	50	☐ Moving in the same city	20
☐ Trouble with your boss	20	☐ Major holiday celebration	15
☐ Losing your job	50	☐ Getting a mortgage	30

TOTAL _____

B. Look at the numbers in the *Points* column. Add up the numbers for all the items you checked. Write the total at the bottom. Is your total above 250? If so, your life is probably very stressful.

C. Write about what you do to reduce the stress in your life.

_____

_____

_____

_____

1

A. Look at the pictures. Check (✓) the correct sentences.

1. ☐ Victor is a political leader.
   ☐ Victor is a successful artist.

3. ☐ Albert is a scientist.
   ☐ Albert is a political leader.

2. ☐ Julia is a writer.
   ☐ Julia is an athlete.

4. ☐ Amy is an athlete.
   ☐ Amy is an artist.

B. Complete the conversation. Use the words in the box.

wealthy	talented	successful	profession	a businessperson

A: In your opinion, what is the best _____?

B: I'm not sure. I want to start my own business. I'm going to be _____.

A: Do you think you're _____ at making money? Are you going to be _____?

B: Well, I think I'm good at making money. And I have a lot of good ideas, so maybe I can become rich.

A: Well, I hope your new business is _____.

B: Thanks!

C. Complete the sentences. Use a word from row A and a word from row B in each answer.

A	stay	history	talented	political	ask	heard
B	of	leaders	home	book	athlete	out

1. Have you _____ _____ Madonna?

2. His name is Joey, and he's very nice. I'm going to _____ him _____.

3. I left my _____ _____ in school.

4. I'm tired. I'm going to _____ _____ today.

5. There are many famous _____ _____ in the United Nations.

6. That soccer player is a _____ _____.

D. Complete the sentences. Use true information.

1. _____ is a well-known political leader.

2. _____ is a successful businessperson.

3. I admire _____ a lot because _____.

4. _____ is my favorite English-language writer.

5. I recently read _____.

6. The person I respect the most is _____.

2

A. Read each answer. Check (✓) the correct question.

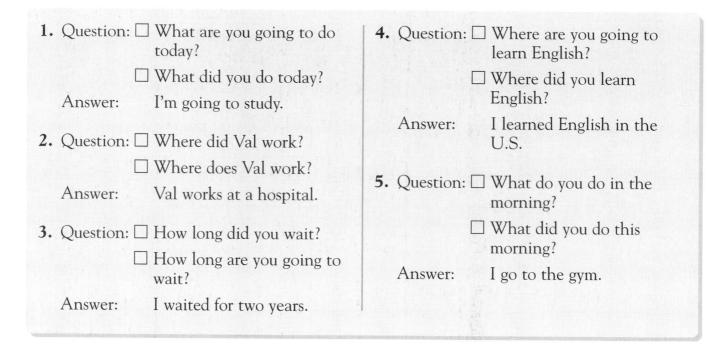

1. Question: ☐ What are you going to do today?
   ☐ What did you do today?
   Answer: I'm going to study.

2. Question: ☐ Where did Val work?
   ☐ Where does Val work?
   Answer: Val works at a hospital.

3. Question: ☐ How long did you wait?
   ☐ How long are you going to wait?
   Answer: I waited for two years.

4. Question: ☐ Where are you going to learn English?
   ☐ Where did you learn English?
   Answer: I learned English in the U.S.

5. Question: ☐ What do you do in the morning?
   ☐ What did you do this morning?
   Answer: I go to the gym.

B. Complete the conversation. Use the correct tense of the verbs in parentheses.

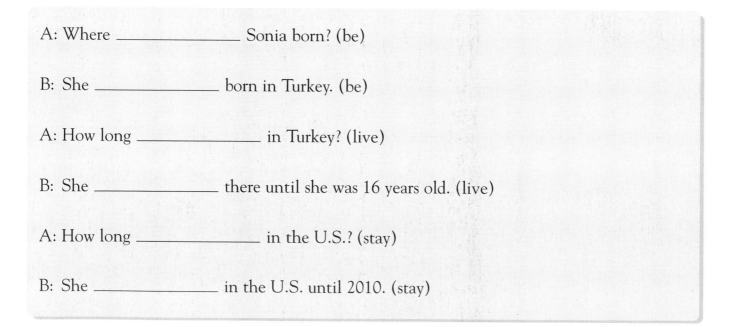

A: Where _____ Sonia born? (be)

B: She _____ born in Turkey. (be)

A: How long _____ in Turkey? (live)

B: She _____ there until she was 16 years old. (live)

A: How long _____ in the U.S.? (stay)

B: She _____ in the U.S. until 2010. (stay)

3

A. Check (✓) the correct response.

1. A: When did your parents leave Colombia?
   B: ☐ They were born in Colombia.
      ☐ I'm not really sure.
   A: You should ask them sometime.

2. A: Is our English teacher a big soccer fan?
   B: ☐ Actually, I have no idea.
      ☐ Nothing special.
   A: Neither do I.

3. A: Have you heard of Macy Gray?
   B: ☐ I'm not really sure.
      ☐ Where does she live?
   A: She's a famous pop singer.

4. A: What's the score?
   B: ☐ Actually, I have no idea.
      ☐ I'm a tennis fan.
   A: I think Chris is winning.

5. A: What are you up to tonight?
   B: ☐ I'm not really sure.
      ☐ Have you seen it?
   A: Why don't we go to a movie?

6. A: Where did you put the newspaper?
   B: ☐ No, I didn't.
      ☐ I don't remember.
   A: It's probably in the kitchen.

B. Complete the conversations. Use the sentences in the box.

Who do you admire?	How are you doing?
He's a famous businessperson.	No, I haven't.
I don't remember.	Actually, I have no idea.
I admire your work a lot.	

1. A: _____
   B: Kofi Annan. Have you heard of him?
   A: Yes. He's a political leader, isn't he?

2. A: What is the salary of the President of the United States?
   B: _____
   A: I think it's about $400,000.

3. A: When was our last English test? Do you remember?
   B: No. _____
   But I think it was about two weeks ago.

4. A: Have you met the new business professor?
   B: _____
   A: I'm going to introduce myself to him.
   _____

5. A: _____
   B: Pretty good. How are you?
   A: Okay.

6. A: Your writing is really creative.
   _____
   B: Thanks.

C. Complete the conversation. For one line, use an expression saying you don't know.

A: Who do you admire?

B: _____

A: Where did she/he grow up?

B: _____

A: Why do you admire her/him?

B: _____

4

A. Read the paragraph and study the chart. Be sure you understand what all the jobs are. Use a dictionary to check the meanings. Write them in your notebook.

Each year, the U.S. Bureau of Labor Statistics makes up a list of the country's fastest-growing professions. They divide the professions into groups based on the amount and type of education required. Here is a sample of some recent statistics:

Amount of education	Fastest-growing job openings
On-the-job training	Home health aides Dental assistants
Associate Degree (two years of college)	Computer technicians Veterinary technicians
Bachelor's Degree (four years of college)	Computer programmers Elementary-school teachers
Master's Degree (five years of college)	Audiologists (Hearing specialists) Drug-abuse social workers

B. Make notes about your future work plans.

What work do you plan to do? _____

How much education do you need? _____

Where can you get the education? _____

How long is it going to take? _____

Where do you want to work? _____

C. Write about your future work plans. Use your notes.

_____

_____

_____

_____

Irregular Simple Past Verbs

Present	Simple Past	Present	Simple Past
be	was/were	lend	lent
become	became	lose	lost
begin	began	make	made
break	broke	meet	met
bring	brought	pay	paid
buy	bought	put	put
catch	caught	read	read
choose	chose	ride	rode
come	came	run	ran
cost	cost	say	said
do	did	see	saw
draw	drew	sell	sold
drink	drank	send	sent
drive	drove	shut	shut
eat	ate	sing	sang
fall	fell	sleep	slept
feel	felt	speak	spoke
fight	fought	spend	spent
find	found	stand	stood
fly	flew	steal	stole
forget	forgot	swim	swam
get	got	take	took
give	gave	teach	taught
go	went	tell	told
grow	grew	think	thought
have	had	throw	threw
hear	heard	understand	understood
hit	hit	wake	woke
keep	kept	wear	wore
know	knew	win	won
leave	left	write	wrote

Notes

Notes

Notes

Credits

ILLUSTRATIONS

Reggie Holladay 2, 14, 15, 26, 27, 33, 35, 44, 47, 50, 64, 68
Bill Petersen 5, 8, 10, 20, 32, 38, 40, 56, 58, 62, 63

PHOTOGRAPHICS CREDITS

7 © PictureNet/CORBIS
11 (*top, left to right*) © Gary Conner/PhotoEdit; © Mauritius/Index Stock Imagery/PictureQuest; (*bottom, left to right*) © John Henley/CORBIS; © Frank Herholdt/Getty Images
13 © ABC/courtesy Everett Collection
17 (*top, left to right*) © David Young-Wolff/PhotoEdit; © Tony Freeman/PhotoEdit; (*middle, left to right*) © Jeff Greenberg/PhotoEdit; © Colin Young-Wolff/PhotoEdit; (*bottom, left to right*) © Phyllis Picardi/Index Stock Imagery; © John A. Rizzo/Getty Images
19 (*left to right*) © Jeff Greenberg/The Image Works; © Haruyoshi Yamaguchi/CORBIS SYGMA; © Andrew Shennan/Getty Images
23 (*top, left to right*) © Jonathan Nourok/PhotoEdit; © Digital Vision/Getty Images; (*bottom, left to right*) © Thinkstock/Getty Images; © Amy Etra/PhotoEdit
25 © David Young-Wolff/PhotoEdit
29 (*top, left to right*) © Bill Aron/PhotoEdit; © SSC/SuperStock; © Ivan Batista/SuperStock; © Lawrence Manning/CORBIS; (*bottom, left to right*) © Digital Vision/SuperStock; © Jiang Jin/SuperStock; © Michael Newman/PhotoEdit; © Digital Vision/Getty Images
31 (*top to bottom*) © Tony Freeman/PhotoEdit; © BananaStock/Robertstock.com
41 (*top, left to right*) © Stewart Cohen/Getty Images; © Peter Hvizdak/The Image Works; (*bottom, left to right*) © Mike Powell/Allsport/Getty Images; © Alan Carey/The Image Works
43 © David Young-Wolff/PhotoEdit
49 © Jose Luis Pelaez/CORBIS
53 (*top, left to right*) © David Young-Wolff/PhotoEdit; © Rhoda Sidney/PhotoEdit; (*bottom, left to right*) © Mathieu Jacob/The Image Works; © Colin Young-Wolff/PhotoEdit
55 © David Raymer/CORBIS
60 (*top to bottom*) © Kent Meireis/The Image Works; © George Shelley/CORBIS; © Brand X Pictures/Getty Images
64 (*top to bottom*) © G K & Vikki Hart/Getty Images; © Digital Vision/Getty Images; © Rob Bartee/SuperStock; © Jeff Greenberg/PhotoEdit
71 (*top, left to right*) © David Young-Wolff/PhotoEdit; © PhotoDisc/Getty Images; (*middle, both*) © BananaStock/Robertstock.com; (*bottle, left to right*) © Topham/The Image Works; © Bill Freeman/PhotoEdit